JIMMY CRICKET

Come 'ere – There's More 2

JIMMY CRICKET
Come 'ere – There's More 2

Letters from me Mammy

Illustrated by

PAUL TREVILLION

A STAR BOOK
published by
the Paperback Division of
W. H. ALLEN & Co Plc

A Star Book
Published in 1988
by the Paperback Division of
W H Allen & Co Plc
44 Hill Street
London W1X 8LB

Copyright © Jimmy Cricket 1988

Printed in Great Britain by
Cox & Wyman Ltd, Reading, Berkshire

ISBN 0 352 32290 X

Grateful acknowledgement is given to Central Independent
Television PLC for the use of photographs and script material.

This book is dedicated to my friend and fellow collaborator Eddie Braben whose ingenious comedy writing talents have brought laughter and happiness to millions.

JIMMY CRICKET

Come 'ere – There's More 2

Dear Jimmy

I hope you can read this letter. I am writing to you with a sore finger as I can't find my pen.

The weather here is glorious, the sun is shining in where the roof used to be.

Your father isn't too happy at the moment. He has a great big boil on the end of his nose and it is throbbing and causing him terrible agony. I have been to the doctor and he has given me some tablets to stop me from laughing.

Your Uncle John had to go the hospital yesterday for one of them tetanus injections. He put his false teeth in his back pocket, sat down and bit himself.

Love
Mammy

Dear Mammy

I was sorry to read about your sore finger. I am writing to you with misgivings. She's a nice lady and is helping me with the spellings. Sorry to hear about the boil on the end of dad's nose. Tell him not to use the pink ointment the doctor gave him the last time. It didn't do his boil any good at all and after three days the end of his finger dropped off.

Uncle John always seems to be having trouble with his false teeth. Do you remember the last time when he broke them? He got very frustrated as it took him two weeks to suck a packet of crisps. The television people are looking after me a treat. They've put me in a lovely hotel, the higher up you go the cheaper it is—I've got a tent on the roof.

Love
  Jimmy

Dear Jimmy

That's good news about the way they are treating you at the television studios. Could you let me know when your new series is coming out as your father and me want to know when to take our holidays. Farmer Benson's cow has died, it just dropped down dead. As you can imagine he was very upset as he was milking it at the time. He was rushed to hospital and it took the surgeon two and a half hours to get the bucket off his head.

Here's something you might find difficult to believe. Last night your father was walking home and he turned into a pub. It's a good trick and not many people can do it. I have sent you one of my home-made cakes.

Love
    Mammy

Dear Mammy

Thank you for the cake, it arrived this morning. The postman who delivered it said he knew it was one of your home-made cakes because he said something about his hernia playing him up again.

Last night I did a charity concert for the Old Age Pensioners, the place was packed with standing room only. I think it must have been the sign outside, it said 'This way for the free soup'.

There was a man on the third row and he was one hundred and three. He died when he was one hundred and two but nobody wanted to tell him in case he got upset. They were very grateful for what I did and they wanted to give me a present but they said that they didn't know how to wrap up a Gorilla.

Love
  Jimmy

Dear Jimmy

I was pleased to read that you have been making the old folk happy. Your grandfather is still taking snuff. Last week he tried out a new brand which was much stronger than the one he usually takes, he took a sniff and sneezed. Your grandmother didn't complain, she just waited with a smile while the firemen got her down off the roof. They're still looking for the cat, the piano's in the back garden and your grandfather's ginger beard is in some woman's house three streets away – she keeps trying to get it to take a saucer of milk. Your father wishes to be remembered to you, he's upstairs wallpapering the cellar.

Love
  Mammy

Dear Jimmy

The chimney sweep came yesterday, and we've found the parrot.

More trouble with the gypsies again. The rubbish lying about, just thrown anywhere, the drunken goings on at night. Complaints have been made and the council says that if it doesn't stop we'll have to move on as the gypsies can't stand much more of it.

Little Tommy next door saw the Nit Nurse at school yesterday. She must have been pleased with him because she gave him a note to give to his mother. Tommy has just joined the Boy Scouts and he is learning how to tie knots. At the moment he is tying sheep shanks, the only trouble is he's doing it with real sheep.

Love
  Mammy

Dear Mammy

I forgot to thank you for sending me the hot water bottle. I'm afraid it isn't much use as when I received it the water had gone cold.

I'm glad to say that the electric blanket you sent is working a treat. Could you switch it off at your end as the bed is getting a bit hot. You'll be glad to hear that things couldn't be better for me with my new television series. I heard today that my Fan Club has swollen, he's got the mumps. Thank you for the sweater that you knitted for me, I'll put it on just as soon as I grow another arm.

Love
  Jimmy

Dear Mammy

I couldn't believe it when I received a letter this morning. I opened it and it was a letter offering me a job in Hollywood! When I read it again it was Halewood, as a paint sprayer in the car body shop.

Word has got around that I do a lot of work for charity. Last night the phone went, I managed to stop it with my foot. It was a man representing a worthy cause and he asked me if I'd care to do a sponsored jump off Nelson's Column. I couldn't refuse him but I did say that I'd only do it this once.

I had to go to see the doctor yesterday for some cough mixture. A man came out of the surgery carrying four wooden legs, he told the doctor he was making a coffee table.

Love
  Jimmy

Dear Jimmy

You know how long I've been complaining to the landlord about the damp in all the bedrooms? Well, at long last he's finally done something about it — he's put the gutters on the inside. And would you believe that at long last we've got central heating installed. Your father met some man down at the pub who said he'd install the pipes in on the cheap. I don't think he knows much about it, all the pipes are in the wrong place. If we want a warm we have to go outside and lean against the wall.

I think I made a terrible mistake in buying your father the sundial he's always wanted. He only had it five minutes and he broke his wrist trying to strap it on.

I went to Bingo last night. Old Mrs Newman who runs the little pet shop got a complete line and she jumped up and shouted 'David Attenborough'.

Love
  Mammy

Dear Jimmy

Mr Kelly has got a wooden leg and he's got himself a very good job. He's working at the local bakery, all he has to do is just walk around and put the holes in the doughnuts.

I've had a letter from your sister Maureen in Australia, she says the heat is something fierce. She said it was 98 degrees in the shade, I wrote back and told her to stay in the sun. She is going off on holiday somewhere in Australia soon. I asked your father if he knew Alice Springs. He said, 'Perhaps they use stronger knicker elastic in Australia?'

I must close now as your father is waiting to cut the grass. Why we can't have lino the same as everyone else I'll never know.

Love
  Mammy

Dear Mammy

I'm glad that our Maureen has settled down in Australia. Do you remember when she first went out and she rang you at home and asked, 'What do you call those things that hop up and down all over the place?' and you said, 'Kangaroos' and our Maureen said, 'The beds are full of them.'

I'm afraid the food isn't very good at this hotel I'm staying in. This morning I went for a walk in the park and the Park Keeper told me off for taking the bread off the ducks. I rang room service last night and the man on the other end of the phone said that I could have one just as soon as it had been built.

Love
Jimmy

Dear Jimmy

Sorry to hear that you're not getting enough to eat. I've told your father that I'll make you one of my Angel Cakes. He said, 'One bite of one of your Angel Cakes and he will be.' I didn't say anything to him as he's in a lot of pain at the moment. Last Sunday he cut his nose opening a tin of peaches. Do you remember that Sunday when you were a little boy and I took you to see your Auntie Norah? When we got back home your father said, 'I've had me tea, the peaches were delicious.' When I looked on the sideboard my goldfish had gone.

I've been asking your father for ages now if we could have a holiday by the seaside, he says we can't afford one. He's done the next best thing, he's nailed a kipper to the mantelpiece and switched the electric fan on.

Love
  Mammy

Dear Mammy

Sorry you haven't been able to have a holiday. I've had a couple of days off, I went to Stratford on Avon, home of the Bard. I asked the guide why he was called the Bard and he said that it was because in his day he was barred out of every pub in Stratford. I visited Shakespeare's house, it was fascinating. I actually sat at the desk where he wrote the very first episode of *Eastenders*. I told the guide that I'd appeared in a Shakespeare play. He said, 'Which one' I said *'King Liar'* he said 'Don't you mean *King Lear*' I said 'No, *King Liar* — I told them I could act.' He saw the funny side, he just laughed and rammed a quill up my nose.

Love
  Jimmy

Dear Jimmy

I'm glad to hear that you've been having a nice time, it's been terrible here. Yesterday the village was swept by a gale. It's the first time the village has been swept in years.

I'm delighted to be able to tell you that at long last your father has redecorated the living room. When you walk in it's a real treat as you feel your feet sinking into the sawdust. You'll be thrilled to bits when you see your old room, your father redecorated that as well. He painted your perch green. Your father is worn out with all the work he has been doing, I think that's why he's been having those dreams again. Last night he dreamt he was eating a giant shredded wheat, and when I woke up this morning half the mattress was missing.

Love
  Mammy

Dear Mammy

I can't wait to see my old room. Do you remember when I was home last and I went back to my old school. All the boys were overjoyed at seeing me. I'll never forget the way they cheered and rattled their tin mugs against the bars.

There is still a chance that I might be going to Hollywood, it all depends on whether or not Daffy Duck gets better. This morning I went jogging in the park and a lot of people recognised me. They shouted 'It's Jimmy Cricket, It's Jimmy Cricket.' I was surprised, I didn't realise the lake was so deep. I went to do another charity show for the Over Sixties last night. When I got there they all said they were 59 and went to the pictures.

Love
  Jimmy

Dear Mammy

I went to the zoo on Sunday. I had to give the attendant a fiver to let me out. I went to look at the Baboon and I never realised that a baboon was bald, then I saw that it was standing on it's head.

The Chimp's tea party was great fun. I got two scones and a cream cake. I didn't like the spiders and all the creepy crawly insects. They weren't in the zoo, they were in the bed at the hotel.

Things are beginning to move for me. Yesterday I went to a recording studio for a voice test for a new pop record. The man in charge listened to me sing and said I'd have nothing to worry about as it would be the only record ever issued where the hole in the middle would be bigger than the record. It will be out in three months and available on prescription at Boot's the chemist.

Love
  Jimmy

AND THERE'S MORE

MILK

31

Dear Jimmy

I'm not surprised that they've asked you to make a record as you've always had a beautiful voice. Do you remember when you sang in the Church Choir and every week your auntie Norah asked if the choir could sing 'Abide With Me' as she was taking in lodgers at the time.

Your uncle John has got himself a job at long last, he's working as the attendant at the local baths, he has to keep an eye on the swimmers. If any of them gets into difficulties in the deep end he writes off for a lifebelt.

Last Saturday was the Local Sports Gala and we had a grand time. Mr Tooley who's 98 won the Over Eighties Competition, he threw his walking stick a yard and a half. Big Tom Poole won the Strong Man Contest, he lifted a shire horse over his head. He won a silver cup and a wheelchair. Putting the shot turned out to be a disaster. Nobody knows where the shot finished up but your father should never have fallen asleep on the grass with his mouth open.

Love
  Mammy

Dear Mammy

I'm glad you had such a good day at the sports gala. Do you remember sports day at my old school when I was a lad? I entered the swimming competition. When I dived into the pool somebody shouted, 'Who threw those braces in?' I was the best at the backstroke, once I got going there was no stopping me, I just couldn't stop and almost got run over outside the Co-op. Happy days – whatever became of her? When I'm not working I still try and keep myself in good nick. Last night I worked on the bar for over an hour, it wasn't easy because it had nuts in.

You've got to be fit to do television as rehearsals are very demanding. This morning we started at nine o'clock and didn't finish until five past. The audience at last night's show was the best ever. He said he'd come again next week if matron forgets to lock his door.

Love
  Jimmy

Dear Jimmy

We had quite a bit of excitement in the village last week. You'll never believe this. Mothercare have opened a new shop here. Within an hour of it opening 48 husbands were in bed with headaches. Young Mrs Reynolds who lives opposite bought a baby bouncer. He's six foot four and knocks the living daylights out of her seven. The local midwife says it'll be good for her business, so she's bought a motor bike. One good thing's come out of it, it's inspired your brother, he's opened a pub called 'Fathercare'. It's a very posh pub. Nobody is allowed in unless they'e wearing a cap, collar and tie. I'm not going again, I felt ridiculous. Even though it's his own son's pub your father has only been once, that was the day it opened. I'm expecting him home a week next Tuesday.

Love
  Mammy

Dear Mammy

I'm thrilled to bits to hear that my brother has opened a pub. He never did like that job as a lighthouse keeper. You've seen the size of that lighthouse, he must have been worn out by the time he'd finished filling it with paraffin oil. Do you remember how grateful to him all the sailors were for keeping the light shining? They even made up a poem in his honour. If I remember rightly it went something like this: *Stout stands the lighthouse upon the rock, made out of concrete and brick. Three cheers for the keeper, said the brave sailor lads, he has to trim the wick.*

I did my little bit for charity again yesterday. I went along to the local hospital and did a show for them. Before I did my act all the patients asked me to sign their plaster casts for them. They were all very pleased and have asked me to go back again next week. I've got to anyway to have the stitches taken out.

Love
   Jimmy

Dear Jimmy

The police called at your brother's new pub the other night and asked him about serving drinks after hours. He said 'Yes' and they all had four pints of lager each. Your father went down to the local Labour Exchange yesterday and asked if he could have a job on the Youth Training Scheme. The clerk said, 'You're a bit old, aren't you? It's only for school leavers.' Your father said, 'Is it my fault if I got kept in?' They gave him a job as a Lollipop Man, it didn't last long and he got the sack. He started on Monday morning and he was taking money off the schoolchildren not let let them cross the road. It was the older boys who really got him into trouble, they clubbed together and gave him five pounds to have the Headmaster knocked over by a milk float. The school is expected to reopen just as soon as they get the Headmaster out of the empty milk churn.

Love
  Mammy

Dear Mammy

I just can't believe what's happened to me! It's fantastic! They've actually got a model of me in the famous waxworks. I went to see it for the first time yesterday. The only thing that puzzles me is that I'm sure there isn't supposed to be a wick standing out of the top of my head.

I've been offered a part in a pantomime 'Cat in a Chemist's Shop'. I'm sure that's not right. Do you remember the first pantomime I ever appeared in and I had to come up through a trap-door? Somebody must have done something wrong because I shot up and found myself in the fish and chip shop next door to the theatre. I got battered. I had my all-red costume on. Some woman in the shop looked at me and said, I'll take that bottle of Raspberry' She picked me up, shook me and my hat blew off.

Love
  Jimmy

Dear Jimmy

Your father has got my heart broke. That man will drive me to bad health. Him and his dreams, somebody should throw a net over him. He's now become such a problem the Samaritans are ringing me up about him. You won't believe what happened last night, he dreamt he was Desperate Dan. He pulled all the nails out of the floorboards with his teeth to bake in a pie, got out of bed and fell through the floorboards.

He went to our local doctor and told him about it, he sent him to see a psychiatrist. The psychiatrist examined your father and said, 'You've got nothing to worry about, you're crackers.' This morning he put all his clothes on back to front, walked out of the door and said, 'Hello.' Last week he dreamt he was Ronnie Corbett. I woke up at half past two in the morning and he was walking up and down under the bed. He's got my heart broke.

Love
  Mammy

Dear Mammy

Sorry to hear about dad. If it's any consolation I have
spoken to one of the top medical men who deals with
this sort of problem every day of his life. He said,
'I shouldn't worry about your father, he's crackers.'
I asked him if there was anything that could be done.
He said that every night when dad gets into bed put
a soaking wet towel wrapped under his chin and tied
loosely at the back. I said, 'Will that cure him?' He
said, 'No, but when he wakes up his neck will be
clean.' Why don't you try asking him to sleep in the
spare room for a week? I believe old Mrs Gormley
three streets away has got one. The psychiatrist also
said you might try putting a bag of frozen peas in
the bed once dad goes off to sleep. That will not only
stop the dreams but it will also wake him up and he
can start getting the dinner ready.

Love
  Jimmy

Dear Jimmy

I don't think I mentioned in my previous letters—they're the ones I sent before I wrote this one—I don't think that I've told you the name that your brother has given to his pub—he's called it 'The Slaughterman's Bijou'. I think it's a grand name with a touch of class. Unfortunately he had a bit of bother there last Saturday night when some man drank too much Pineapple Juice and started knocking chunks off the barman. It was the same man who the previous Saturday night drank six pints of orange juice and said he'd fight any man who said that he wasn't Max Jaffa.

Your father was in the pub the other afternoon and he at a Ploughman's Lunch. The Ploughman got very annoyed and he made your father buy him anothr one. Your brother is now serving Sunday lunches. We went and had our Sunday lunch there last Saturday to avoid the crowd on the following day. Your father had roast duck, I don't think it had been cooked properly as it kept eating the peas off the plate.

Love
  Mammy

Dear Mammy

I think that the name 'The Slaughterman's Bijou' is very sophisticated. He always was a man of the world with a touch of quality. Do you remember when he used to go into the local he always asked for a 'Workingman's Cocktail'. That's a pint of brown ale with a cow heel in it.

I ate out last night for a change, I thought I'd try one of those Indian restaurants, I had Chicken Lips on Toast. Never again, I hate toast. The waiter was a very nice man. He told me that on feast days in his country they roasted an elephant. When it was eaten it took 28 men to pull the wishbone. He told me that they had a fracas in the restaurant the previous night. I said to him, 'The next time you have one let me know and I'll try it with chips.' I didn't go out to eat last Sunday like you and dad did, I stayed in and had a frozen dinner for one. I'll reply to the previous letters you sent me just as soon as they arrive.

Love
  Jimmy

Dear Jimmy

I've some grand news about your Cousin Joe. Last Thursday he broke the world record for the 500 yards. He did five hundred yards in ten seconds with his clogs on. It happened at work when he wasn't looking where he was going and he fell down the lift shaft. I'm glad to say that he didn't hurt himself until he landed at the bottom.

The other day I held a coffee morning to raise money so that I can hold other coffee mornings, it's much cheaper that way. The other day the Salvation Army came around the village giving away second-hand clothing and your father got himself rigged out for nothing. He doesn't mind the bonnet but he thinks the skirt will need leting out a few inches. You know that great big fat woman opposite, Mrs Tyson, she got a free pair of corsets off the Salvation Army. Ever since she's had them on she's been been going around singing 'All is safely gathered in'. Sorry to hear that you haven't received my previous letters. I'll write them tomorrow.

Love
  Mammy

Dear Mammy

Thank you for your previous letter which has just arrived. Last night on the show we had a man who did the most amazing and daring trick I have ever seen. He dived into a tank full of those ferocious Piranah fish, the deadliest fish in the world. Every body said it was the most amazing trick they'd ever seen, even his widow was delighted.

I had a few days off yesterday and I visited a stately home. The architects in those days were perfectionists, I don't know how they did it. Every room I went into, the floor just reached my feet. The guide told us that the relics hanging from the beam in the great hall belonged to a 16th-century acrobat who should have had more sense.

In the main bedroom was the largest bed in the world. The man said that when it was in use it took sixteen chambermaids to empty the hot-water bottle. Sir Walter Raleigh had stayed there, you could see the scratch marks on the wall where he left his bike.

Love
  Jimmy

Dear Jimmy

I was glad to read in your previous letter which came next week that you had a nice day out. We've got the damp back again in the upstairs rooms. Last night your father climbed into bed and a duck bit him, he just rolled in agony for over an hour, it's a terrible thing to see a duck rolling in agony. We showed the landlord the damp patch on the bedroom wall, he said it wasn't a damp patch. According to him the local river is making a detour. I think he believed us when a mouse ran across the room wearing wellies.

As you know, your brother is now serving meals at his pub 'The Slaughterman's Bijou'. The other day he had a bit of a problem because a coach-load of forty people arrived unexpectedly, all wanting something to eat. All your brother had was a large trifle — he clouted it with a plank and everybody got a bit. Your father went to the doctor's yesterday and said to him, 'Can you give me anything for gallstones, doctor?' He gave him a catapult. The doctor gave him a bottle. He said, 'When the pain gets very bad get your wife to hit you over the head with it.' This is the previous letter which I shall post next week so that you can catch up on the other letters which I'll post tomorrow.

Love
  Mammy

Dear Mammy

Don't send me any more previous letters as I now have 300 of them. It is a beautifully sunny day and I am writing this letter sitting on the tiny balcony of my hotel room. Oooooh! I am now writing this letter on the pavement outside the hotel. I think I've hurt myself in the process, which is something of a surprise as I didn't even know that I had one.

Last night in the hotel I fancied something different and I asked the waitress for a plate of blubber. She said, 'Blubber?' I said, 'You get it from whales.' She said, 'I'm not going all that way.' The man sitting at the next table had a plate of snails. He ate them all and it took him three and a half hours to get to the exit, and he left a silver trail across the carpet. First thing this morning I fed the birds in my dressing gown, how they got in there in the first place I'll never know.

Love
  Jimmy

Dear Jimmy

Now I've heard everything! The cheek of the man! Your father has asked me to buy a second-hand car so that I can drive him to drink.

A Gipsy called here yesterday selling artificial flowers, your father took a bunch off him and gave him an artificial pound note. The Gipsy got very angry and shouted through the letter box, 'I'll put a curse on you.' Your father just laughed, turned around and tripped over his tail.

We had a lovely day out yesterday at the local flower show, but it was very hot and my feet were giving me gyp. I sat down and took my shoes off because my bunions were throbbing. One of the judges must have been short-sighted because he looked at them and gave me a 'First' in the Home Grown Radishes Section.

Your Uncle John didn't have such a good day, he had to be rushed to hospital. Serves him right for trying to smell a Venus Fly Trap. They've got him in a bed in the main car park as they couldn't get his nose through the entrance doors to the hospital. He sneezed and dented a surgeon's Mercedes.

Love
  Mammy

Dear Mammy

It was good to hear that you enjoyed the flower show. This morning I went for a walk through Hyde Park. It's a lovely park and is named after the man who who designed it, Sir Alf Park. They have a clock in the park and it's made out of flowers, when I looked at it it was twenty-five past Daffodil. I think it was a bit slow, according to my watch it was half past Mickey Mouse. I went to Number Ten Downing Street and the Prime Minister was standing on the front step with an Arab man. She didn't look too happy, something to do with oil deliveries, it's a big house to keep warm and she must be freezing. The Prime Minister drove off in a big car, she was going to play draughts because the man standing next to me said she was off to Chequers for the weekend. The man wouldn't let me into the House of Commons. He said I'd only upset the comedians who were already in there.

Love
  Jimmy

Dear Jimmy

It was nie to hear about the flowers in Hyde Park. I'm ashamed of our garden, not a blade of grass and the soil is as hard as iron. Yesterday I had to go out with a Black and Dekker and drill holes so that the worms could come up for air. The front garden is only small but I look after it myself and it's beautiful. In fact it's so nice I've brought it in and put it in the best room.

Your father's not in at the moment, he's gone to get all the shopping in from the Supermarket before they open. He was up early this morning and brought the milk in from next door's front step. He was thrilled last week because he thought there might be the chance of a job on the milk float. Unfortunately he didn't get the job as the horse made an unexpected recovery.

He did a stupid thing yesterday. The Rent Man knocked at the front door and your father shouted, 'We've gone on our holidays.'

Love
   Mammy

Dear Mammy

I've had a letter from Aunt Norah and she told me how Uncle John had raised fifty pounds for charity when he took part in a sponsored 'lie in'. He went to bed on Sunday and forced himself to stay there until Thursday afternoon. He's a good man.

Now that the weather has turned a bit colder I went to buy myself some warm clothing. The man in the shop took my inside leg measurement. I wouldn't have minded but I only wanted a scarf.

The people at the television studios have been very nice to me, I have my own place in the car park. It's only for the time being, I can have a dressing room the same as everyone else as soon as one becomes empty. Thanks for sending me the plus fours you made yourself out of two empty Hoover bags. They fit grand, the only trouble is every time I breathe in my shirt flies off.

I might take up golf as soon as I've saved up enough money to buy a racquet.

Love
  Jimmy

Dear Jimmy

Young Tommy from next door came in to see us last night, he's worrying about his GCE exams. Your father told him not to worry too much as he had passed the GCE. Tommy was very surprised and said, 'You've passed the General Certificate of Education?' Your father said, 'Oh, I though it meant Guinness Certificate of Europe.' I had a wonderful day out yesterday with all the other ladies from the Women's Institute, it was grand. We all went around to the Men's Institute and smashed all their windows. We finished up at the Village Hall with an Afternoon Tea Dance. I had four cucumber sandwiches and six dances during the 'Excuse Me' quickstep. When I got back home your father had been at the drink again. I could tell because as I walked in he was trying to get the tortoise to beg for a lettuce leaf. The tortoise got very angry and bit your father's ankle.

Love
    Mammy

Dear Mammy

It's happened. I was sitting in a serve-yourself cafe last night and I saw 'Her'. She was sitting at the next table to mine, just one look and I felt a lump in my throat, I'd swallowed the plastic teaspoon. You know how hopeless I am with girls, I got all flustered and said all the wrong things when we got talking. She said, 'My name's Sylvia.' I said, 'That's a strange coincidence, that's my father's name.' I don't think that was right somehow. She had the most beautiful, perfect teeth I've ever seen, I saw them for a second when she opened her handbag. I bought her a doughnut, she left the hole – she said she'd just had her tea. She had the most perfect shaped nose I have ever seen. I sighed and asked her if she had another. She said, 'No, it's the only nose I've got'. She's a bit special and I'm seeing her again quite soon. I think she recognised me because when we left she asked the manager if there was a back way out. I'll tell you more about her in my next letter.
Love
  Jimmy

Dear Jimmy

I'm a bit worried about you going out with this girl. I've had a word with your father and asked him if he's had a man to man talk with you about life. He said that he did tell you that Snow White was only a cartoon. He didn't want to mention Father Christmas to you as you were only 25 at the time. I know you say that she comes from a good family and her father must be a man of great importance if he is the British Ambassador to Stockton-on-Tees. I'd like to know a lot more about this girl. Is she the same as yourself or is she normal? You are very innocent, son. I remember when you were nineteen and you asked me if you'd have to marry Sheila because you'd had a ride on her bike. I want you to find out more about this girl before you get too involved. Remember that love is like a bike, any old thing will do to learn on, but when you get one get a good one.

Love
   Mammy

Dear Mammy

Thank you for the advice. Dad did have a talk to me and I still haven't got over Snow White. What was it that he wanted to tell me about Father Christmas? I still write to him every Christmas and he hasn't let me down yet, except last year when I didn't get the two-seater executive jet plane, but I can wait.

Sylvia is a very good living girl. She told me herself that she goes to church every time she gets christened. Her mother's a countess. She must be because her father's an accountant. She has the most beautiful brown eyes you have ever seen, every time I look at them it reminds me of the time when I bought those two tins of creosote to do the fence back home. She comes from a very wealthy family because at least once a month they go off to a villa, I know it's Aston Villa but what difference does that make. I'll be able to tell you more after I've taken her out tonight.

Love
   Jimmy

Dear Jimmy

You've got me very worried. Your father is worried sick, he hasn't slept a wink all afternoon. You're beginning to sound more like one of them big city Men of the World'. The next thing you know you'll be crossing the road on your own. I'm not happy about the sound of this girl, for all you know she could be after your money. Don't let her see your Building Society Book, there's twelve pounds 75p in it, with the interest to go on top of that.

Not much has happened back home, except for the strike at the Candle Factory. All the workers are asking for a shorter working wick. I've lost my reading glasses, I've only got my distance glasses. Your father has to go and stand on the other side of the street with the paper open so's I can read the news. Young Tommy says that if he doesn't pass his GCE he'll run away from home and get a job on one of them Oil Rugs. Let me know how you go on with this young woman of yours.

Love
  Mammy

Dear Mammy

It's all over. You and my dad can stop worrying
because I won't be seeing Sylvia again. I've only ever
seen her at night, yesterday I met her in broad daylight
and I couldn't believe my eyes — she's green! Then
she told me the truth, she's a dipper in a dye factory.
Can you imagine what might happen if I married a
green woman? We could well have green children,
we'd have to sit them in the window to colour up.
It's finished. I wasn't too happy the first time I took
her to the pictures. I took her home and it was pitch
dark, she said, 'You can kiss me goodnight if you
want to.' I bent down in the dark and I said to her,
'Your lips are cold.' She said, 'That's the letter box.'
If I got nothing else from the romance at least I've
got a new joke for my act. I'll wait until I meet a
woman like you.

Love
  Jimmy

Dear Jimmy

That was a lovely letter. I told your father that you said you'd wait until you met a woman like me. I belted him one when he said, 'Tell him to try the nearest Pet Shop.' We tried that new Chinese Take-Away that's just opened in the village. I'm glad we went, the till looks nice on the sideboard. I was watching one of those travel films on the TV the other night and it was all about China. There were a lot of people riding in what they call Rickshaws, the funny thing was all the horses in China look like men. Nearly all the people were living on boats. I wished we lived on a boat, our rent man called, we forgot it was him and we opened the door. He said, 'I don't believe it! It's been ages.' We pretended to look surprised when he told us that Hitler was dead. I said I wouldn't pay him a ha'penny until he'd got rid of the damp. He said that was just an excuse and the house wasn't damp. He soon changed his mind when I took him into the front room to watch your father feeding the seals.

Love
  Mammy

Dear Mammy

Great news. I've been offered a job making a
commercial for television. It could be the easiest
money I've earned in my life. All I've got to do is
run down a garden and make sure the toilet roll
doesn't tear. They asked me to do a commercial for
a new aftershave called Mustang. The man said, 'Try
it out for yourself for a day or two and see what you
think of it.' So I did. I put the Mustang aftershave
on and four donkeys followed me back to the hotel.

Hammer Films who make all those horror pictures
invited me to go for a test in a new spine-chilling
thriller, but I didn't get the part. When I walked into
the studio Christoper Lee looked at me and passed
out.

We had a sword swallower on the show last night,
he swallowed a six-foot sword. The only trouble was
he's only five foot three and he was pinned to the
floor for three hours. And an American couple, he
shot a cigarette out of his wife's mouth. He wasn't
supposed to, they're singers and they were having
a barney in the dressing room.

Love
  Jimmy

Dear Jimmy

The other day I went to a Whist Drive. I can't play Whist but I thought the drive might do me good. I don't think the other people there liked me very much as they kept getting up and moving to another table.

The ice-cream van pulled up in the street yesterday and your granddad bought himself a stick of candy floss. He said, 'I haven't had one of these for years.' He was like a child, he really enjoyed it until it was all gone then he was very upset—his beard was missing! You remember that Cuckoo Clock that your grandmother has had on her kitchen wall? It's been in the family for over a hundred years and is getting a bit the worse for wear. Every hour it pops it's head out and says, 'Have you got any snuff?'

I went to one of them car boot sales with your father last Thursday. We bought the boot, when we've saved up enough money we'll buy the rest of the car.

Love
  Mammy

Dear Mammy

The weather has turned a bit cold. Last night there was a ground frost, I think I'll sleep in the bed tonight. There's a man staying in the same hotel as me and he's the leading violinist with The London Symphony Orchestra. The other night he went to the Royal Albert Hall for a symphony concert and he must have got the dates mixed up because he got knocked out in the first round by Frank Bruno.

I got weighed the other day and I was a couple of pounds over my normal weight so I decided to start doing proper exercises. I bought myself one of them rowing machines. It wasn't much good, I'd only gone a couple of yards and it sank. The food at this hotel is much better than the food I used to get when I stayed in those cheap digs years ago. In those days whenever I saw the landlady's husband cutting the privet I knew we were going to have salad for tea. Still, I won't be staying at places like that again until I've finished, clapped out and nobody wants me-next week probably.

Love
  Jimmy

Dear Jimmy

We've had a terrible worry here at home. Your little Uncle John went missing for three days, not a sight of him anywhere. The police were going to bring in tracker dogs until your Aunt Norah found him when she emptied the Hoover bag. He had to spend two days in hospital suffering from Severe Fluffitis.

We're thinking about going abroad for a holiday. Your father and me went to see the travel agent and he had the Brochures, the poor man must have been in agony. We asked him what was the cheapest holiday abroad that he had, he said, 'Spain and back for ten pounds.' I knew there'd be a catch in it somewhere, we have to supply our own oars. I want to go to Italy because I'd love to see all those tulips and the windmills. Your father says he'd like to go to Malta because a man in the pub told him that the Maltesers were very nice people. We'll think about it.

Love
 Mammy

Dear Mammy

I'm glad you're thinking about a holiday as you deserve one. Why don't you go back to Scotland? You both enjoyed it the last time that you went. Do you remember when you went on a tour of the distillery and dad slipped and fell into that great big vat of whisky. He shouted 'Save me, Save me, a week next Thursday.' If I remember, you got very angry with the American lady tourist at Loch Ness when she asked you if you'd mind going for a paddle in the lake so as she could take a photo. Have you thought about a holiday camp? There's always plenty to do. Every night they play Squash — ten people to one chalet. There's all-in-wrestling every day, it's the only way you can get your dinner. If you remember I began my show business career working at a holiday camp. I wasn't all that keen on being a chalet maid but at least it was a start. Thanks for the photo of the garden. The concrete gnome sets it off a treat.

Love
  Jimmy

Dear Jimmy

The concrete gnome was a photo of your father pulling the weeds up. We've decided where we're going on our holidays this year, Scarborough because it's not far from the home of The Brontë Sisters, and I've still got their record of 'Don't sit under the apple tree with anyone else but me.' Your sister Maureen has written and invited us to go and stay with her in Australia. I don't fancy going, it's such a terrible long journey and I believe you have to get four buses. I'd love to see our Maureen but I don't think I'd like to stay in her house because she hasn't even got a bathroom put in yet. Every time she writes to me she says that her husband is out in the bush. And your father isn't all that keen, he says he'd be scared to death in case he got biten by one of them Boomerangs.

Love
  Mammy

Dear Mammy

I've started taking driving lessons. I had my first lesson this morning and as I've never driven a car before I was a bit nervous. I got into the car and the instructor said to me, 'If you sit in the front you'll find it much easier to reach the steering wheel.' I sat in the front and the instructor said, 'Have you looked in the mirror?' I said to him, 'I haven't had time to read a paper this morning.' He said, 'Have you got anything behind you?' I said, 'I've got a few bob in the Building Society.' He didn't seem very impressed with this. He asked me which gear I'd be starting off in. I said, 'The gear I'm wearing now.' For a trained driving instructor he seems very nervous for some reason. I'll let you know how I get on when I write you my next letter which will be the one after this.

Love
  Jimmy

Dear Jimmy

You be careful when you're taking them motor lessons. I can still remember what you were like when I bought you your first three-wheeler bike. You kept falling off it—in the end you gave it up and walked to work. You're as bad as your father when it comes to mechanical gadgets. Do you remember when he bought me a washing machine? When it was delivered he made the men take it back to the shop because he said there was no water in it. It was the same with the first electric fire we ever bought. He was sitting in his armchair, he gave the electric fire a poke and finished up at the bottom of next door's garden.

When you're taking them motor lessons watch out for pedestrians—or people of any other religion come to that. Let me know how you get on as I'm very worried. If you can't cope I can still send you your old roller skates, but remember this time, you don't put your socks on over them.

Love
   Mammy

Dear Mammy

You've got nothing to worry about as I'm doing grand with the driving lessons. The driving instructor is a nice man and very religious. Every time He gets into the car with me he takes his rosary beads out. I had my second lesson today and he told me to drive in reverse. I did try but I had to tell him that it was impossible as I couldn't get at the steering wheel sitting with my back to it. The car I'm learning in is what they call a Bullnose. It was a Ford Escort until I drove into the wall. It's one of those cars with the engine in the back, it was at the front until I hit the lampost. The instructor is a pale-faced man with grey hair. I can't understand that as he had a good colour and a shock of red hair when I first met him. I did my very first reverse this morning and the driving instructor couldn't believe it. He said it was the first time he'd ever seen anyone drive a car of this size backwards into a telephone box. The man who was using the telephone at the time couldn't believe it either. I think there'll be more.

Love
  Jimmy

Dear Jimmy

I've more to worry about than your motor lessons at the moment. Your father is in terrible mood. The other day he went sea fishing and he caught what he thought was a monster eel — British Telecom went mad! He'd pulled up the Trans-Atlantic telephone cable. I'm shattered. I went to see the doctor and he's given me something to steady my nerves, it's called 'A Cave in the Hills'.

I had an early night last night and went to bed with a book. Your father had gone to your brother's pub, The Slaughterman's Bijou. He said that he wanted to make sure that he ran out of draught Guinness. When he got home a bit the worse for drink he shouted, 'Where are you?' I shouted back, 'I'm in bed with John Steinbeck.' Your father roared, 'The dirty dog, I'll kick his teeth in!' He was no better this morning. He said he was cold, I told him to light the firewood, he said it was damp and he'd been twenty minutes trying to get it to light. I came downstairs and all the celery had gone. Be careful in that motor.

Love
    Mammy

Dear Mammy

I'm very upset. This morning I went for my driving lesson at the usual place but it was closed down. The man who has the place next door said that the driving instructor had to sell up shortly after he was carried off in a van screaming about some terrible man who'd been sent by the devil to punish him. I wonder what the poor man meant? He's such a nice man I decided to go and see him in the hospital. I found him on the lawn sitting in a wheelchair. I offered to wheel him around the grounds and he leapt out of the chair, over a ten-foot wall and nearly got run over by a number 74 bus. The man must have had some sort of terrible experience to get himself in a state like that. I've decided to forget all about the car, after all I've had my legs all my life and they haven't had to have one MOT.

Love
  Jimmy

Dear Jimmy

I've got a lot to be thankful for—your father isn't speaking to me. It was because of what happened at breakfast yesterday morning when your father said to me, 'I can't eat this porridge, it's full of lumps.' I had to tell him it was my fault—my beads broke.

I met Mrs Mullen in the corner shop and she asked how you were. I told her that you were the same as always. She was very kind and told me not to cry. I prefer the little corner shop to the supermarket, it's more homely. It's nice to go in the shop and see the cat sitting on the boiled ham. Mr Connors who runs the corner shop says that he's not going to sell any more imported bacon from overseas. He said the other night he was getting into the bath and he had Danish' written all down his left side. June Noon got married yesterday, she got married in white. The groom had to wait at the church for three and a half hours while the Snowcem dried.

Love
  Mammy

Dear Mammy

I remember June Noon. She was the girl who said I was the best-looking lad in the village the day before she started wearing bi-focals.

A man jumped on me last night as I was walking home from the TV studios. He took my wallet with my card in it that I use for getting money from the bank. It's got Stick 'Em Up' printed on it. I went to the local police station to report it and the Sergeant knew who I was, he said he was a fan. What did surprise me was that he was even a bigger fan of my dad because he had his picture on the wall. While I was at the TV studios I met that weather forecaster you like, Michael Fish. He breathes through his ears—he was in the canteen having an ants egg sandwich. I said to him, 'Lovely day.' He said, 'Not so loud. It's supposed to be snowing.' I had a peep into the newsroom, that was interesting. Sandy Gall was recording the news for next week—he's going on holiday.

Love
  Jimmy

Dear Jimmy

I'm near demented! Your father has got me persecuted! He's started again having those dreams of his. No woman should be made to suffer like this. Last night he dreamt he was Steve Davis in the World Snooker Finals. When I woke up at half past three this morning he was sitting in the pocket of his dressing gown hanging on the door and shouting, 'Foul shot.' I had to chalk the end of the broom and poke him out. I sent for the doctor and he examined your father. He took me to one side and said, 'I'm afraid it's very serious. If he loses the next frame he's out of the competition.' I couldn't believe it! I smiled, thanked the doctor and shoved the end of the broom up his nose. His eyes are glued to the television all day and when there's snooker on he talks about nothing else, thinks about nothing else. Now when he has a boiled egg he chalks the spoon first. I'm packing a suitcase, the darts are on all next week.

Love
  Mammy

Dear Mammy

Sorry to hear about dad and his snooker. All this snooker talk must be getting you down, you need a break. Oops, Sorry! All my fans were in to see the show last night. They couldn't clap when I came on because they were all wearing jackets with very long sleeves that were strapped up at the back. I did my juggling act with six balls, I finished with five – it was my own fault for having my mouth open. I did my new joke, the one about the housewife who accidentally swallowed half a bottle of bleach. When her husband rang the hospital to ask how she was the doctor said, 'Fair'. Some man in the audience laughed, but he was thrown out because they don't allow drunks in. When I came out a lady asked for a photo of me for her son. I was very flattered until she said she wanted him to see it so that he could find out what could happen to him if he didn't pass his 'O' Levels. My Fan Club should have had a meeting last night only there was somebody in the telephone box. They were very disappointed and left on their tandem.

Love
  Jimmy

Dear Jimmy

It was your Uncle John's and Aunt Norah's wedding anniversary today, they received a lovely telegram from the British Boxing Board of Control. They've been married for forty-three years and your Uncle John still calls her 'Sweetmeat'. He can't remember her first name. I don't know what they call it when you've been married for forty-three years. I know it's not Silver, Diamond or Pearl. Your Aunt Norah thinks it's called Purgatory. They had a lovely party with a running buffet — we had to, it was the only way we could catch the meat pies. Your Aunt Norah looked a treat, she had her hair in a bun and her nose in a crab sandwich. After a few drinks your Uncle John got all overcome and sang 'Girl of My Dreams I Love You'. Your Aunt Norah cried as he was singing it to the woman from next door. The room was packed tight with people and your father played his accordion. He got thrown out for pinching sixteen girls at the same time.

Love
  Mammy

Dear Mammy

I was very pleased to hear that you enjoyed yourselves
at the party. I remember when you and dad had your
wedding anniversary, you held it at the Co-op. We
never did find out who turned the handle when dad
was sitting on the bacon slicer. I remember that it
all ended in a terrible barney when somebody asked
my dad if he'd like a drop of the hard stuff. He said,
'I would that' and a brick fell on his head. I'll never
forget it because I didn't realise that I had so many
aunties and uncles. Every one of them patted me on
the head and gave me a sixpence. When I was going
home people were looking at me and saying, 'Who's
that rich midget?' I've still got the photograph taken
on the day you and dad got married. Dad looking very
proud in his naval uniform. How long was he in the
WRENS? I'm only kiddin'.

Love
  Jimmy

Dear Jimmy

I am writing this letter and keeping my eye on your father's dinner at the same time. I've got a sheep's head in the oven and it keeps opening the door and saying, 'Excuse me, have you got such a thing as a glass of water?' Your father said that nobody can cook one like me, he often says that he married me for my sheep's head. I was reading about you in the Sunday paper, we're all very proud of you, son. It must be nice to be 'abysmal'. Your cousin Joe came around last Thursday, he'd been unconscious since Wednesday. What happened was he was sitting in the back garden under the cherry tree and a tin of shoe polish fell and hit him on the head. I had to buy some ointment — from Boots.

Love
   Mammy

Dear Mammy

Guess what? I saw Anneka Rice today! I have never seen a woman with so much energy. She jumped out of a helicopter with a map in her hand and was dashing around all over the place asking people questions. She jumped back into the helicopter, flew off then jumped out again to ask more people directions. It was amazing! She wasn't doing a television programme — she'd forgotten where she lived.

I ate out last night at the cafe across the road. I sat next to a cross-eyed man and he ate my sausage, egg and chips. I said to the waitress, 'What's the Chef's Speciality?' She said, 'Standing on his head and whistling up the left leg of his trousers.' I had some apple pie. It wasn't like your home-made applie pie — you could eat it. I'm only jokin', Mammy. Do you remember the time when my dad read in the newspaper that eighty per cent of accidents happen in the kitchen? You hit him with the rolling pin when he said, 'But why do we have to eat them?'

Love
  Jimmy

Dear Jimmy

You know the young couple opposite? Well, he got himself into terrible trouble with his wife the other night, and you know what an enormous girl she is. He got home a bit the worse for drink and she was standing on the front step in her vest waiting for him. He looked at her and said, 'Hello, somebody's whitewashed the outside of the house.' It's a lovely house, it's got twelve acres. Her father left it to her. He was a dentist.

You remember Mr Connors from just down the street? He's had the sack from the motor car factory for not putting the faults in.

Wouldn't you think that a man of your grandfather's age would have more sense? He's entered for the milk race—he was out yesterday practising and he fell off the cow. He fell with a terrible bump and buckled his snuff box.

Love
  Mammy

Dear Mammy

I got into trouble with the waitress in the television canteen at tea-time. I said to her 'That lettuce looks nice and crisp and green.' She said, 'That's the boiled ham.' The poor woman, she's got ten children and she only gets ten pounds a week. I said to her, 'How do you manage to make ends meet?' She said, 'My husband's a contortionist.' I sat next to a very nice girl who's just come back from a holiday in Spain. She said that somebody pinched her bottom. The Spanish police are going to send it on to her as soon as they find it. She told me that she smokes two hundred cigarettes a day but fortunately it hasn't become a habit.

By the way, if my dad's going to repair the roof you'd better remind him of the price of lead — it's now eighteen months a hundredweight. A lady came up to me in the hotel last night and said, 'I wonder if you'd mind giving me your autograph when you've finished washing the dishes.'

Love
  Jimmy

Dear Jimmy

Something very odd happened in the village recently. You know the big posh house up on the hill? Well, last week they added another wing and two days later it flew away. The head gardener has left and found another job, he now holds a very important post at the dogs home. It was a beautiful house, if you stood in the garden you could see eaves jutting out — she was a big girl. When the Squire died he left the house to his son the squirrel.

We had a terrible accident here yesterday. A bread van took the bend too quickly and crashed into the blacksmith's who was very busy with a roaring fire going at the time. The police had to divert all the traffice for three hours as the road was blocked with toast.

Love
  Mammy

Dear Mammy

You'll never guess who I bumped into yesterday, Kenny O'Brien, he went to the same school as me. He had a good job here in London, only the poor man got the sack on the first day. He was working for Securicor and somebody nicked the van. You remember his mother, a great big fat lady. She did a good job during the war, she was a road block. If you remember, his dad was always in trouble. Do you remember that time he was up in court on a charge? I thought the judge was a bit severe with the sentence, he gave him three years for dancing. I suppose it was his own fault for waltzing off with the Christmas Club money. They were a terrible family for borrowing, always knocking at the front door asking for things. 'Have you got a cup of sugar? Could you let us have a bottle of milk? Could you put some soap on this wet flannel?' Nobody's perfect. How about that time my father was sitting on the sofa with his arm around you and singing, 'I love the dear silver that shines in your purse.' It's a funny old life.

Love
  Jimmy

JIMMY: Mammy!

MAMMY: Jimmy!

JIMMY: My mammy's name isn't Jimmy.

MAMMY: Who do you want?

JIMMY: My mammy.

MAMMY: This isn't Miami.

JIMMY: It's me, Jimmy.

MAMMY: You shouldn't be wasting your money on a phone call, son.

JIMMY: I won't if the string doesn't break. Where's dad?

MAMMY: He's in the garden.

JIMMY: What's he growing?

MAMMY: Tired.

JIMMY: How's his rhubarb?

MAMMY: It'll be stone cold by the time he comes in.

JIMMY: I'll have to dash. I'll give you a ring next week.

MAMMY: I've got a ring. Try telephoning me.

JIMMY: Bye.

JIMMY: Mammy!

MAMMY: Jimmy!

JIMMY: I haven't got long.

MAMMY: I didn't know you were that ill.

JIMMY: I've never felt better.

MAMMY: The budgie's dead.

JIMMY: Where did it happen?

MAMMY: The cat won't tell us. Your Uncle John's got another set of false teeth.

JIMMY: He must have had about three dozen sets of false teeth in the past year.

MAMMY: I know. He's building a rockery. How are the shows going?

JIMMY: Great. The manager of the theatre said that I've done for comedy what Captain Ahab did for Save the Whale.

MAMMY: That's nice, son.

JIMMY: The pips have gone.

MAMMY: They'd steal anything over there.

JIMMY: Bye.

JIMMY:	Hello!
MAMMY:	Hello!
JIMMY:	Is that the woman my dad married?
MAMMY:	Yes. Who are you?
JIMMY:	Jimmy.
MAMMY:	There's a coincidence! I married your father.
JIMMY:	Did my dad go to see the doctor about his warts.
MAMMY:	This morning.
JIMMY:	What did the doctor say?
MAMMY:	He said, 'Go out the back way, people might think I'm a vet.'
JIMMY:	How are you keeping?
MAMMY:	I haven't been able to get out of the chair for three days.
JIMMY:	Why's that?
MAMMY:	Your father tied the knots very tight.
JIMMY:	I've got to dash.
MAMMY:	Ring me next week.
JIMMY:	Can I reverse the call?
MAMMY:	I won't be able to understand a word if you're talking backwards.
JIMMY:	It doesn't matter. Bye.

Dear Jimmy

I'm sorry to have to write with bad news. Your little Uncle John is in hospital. I did warn him. He was here the other day playing with your old train set and he fell out of the guard's van. He's such a little man—he's the only man I know who has to jump up to smell a Dwarf Tulip.

He's started again, your father. He had another of his dreams last night, he frightened the life out of me, he dreamt he was the Hunchback of Notre Dame. I woke up at two o'clock this morning, he was standing on the front doorstep with the tortoise stuck up the back of his nightshirt, ringing the doorbell like a madman and shouting, 'Let me in, Esmeralda!' The doctor gave me a prescription. I took it to the chemist and he gave me a mallet. I used it last night because I was out of patience with the man. I woke up at twenty past three, your father was dreaming that he was an ostrich and he was eating my curlers. I hit him with the mallet, he just laughed and flew up onto the roof.

Love
    Mammy

Dear Mammy

I'm sorry to hear about the upset you're having with
my dad and his dreams. I think I've found the answer.
Why don't you tell him to go for a long walk before
he goes to bed and while he's out move to another
house.

I've been jotting down some of the funny things
that used to happen when I was living at home. Do
you remember the day when that old man knocked
at the front door with a wooden leg and he fell over
backwards? Then there was the time when you and
my dad had that terrible barney, I'll never forget it
if I live to be normal. You'd worked for months doing
a beautiful embroidery saying 'Home Sweet Home'.
Dad had it framed and hung it up in the house next
door. Remember the night grandad got drunk? He
came home, put the tortoise on his head and tried to
give his bowler hat a lettuce leaf. That Christmas
when I went carol singing, I went to this great big
house in the dark and I was soaked, sang one carol
and the man gave me five pounds. He said, 'You
deserve it, son. This is a lighthouse.' It's a funny old
life.

Love
  Jimmy

Dear Mammy

I haven't forgotten grandfather's birthday which is on February the fourteenth of August. It falls on a Friday and so does grandfather after the drink. I am sending him some 'Snuff Vouchers'. I'll need twelve and up to now I've only collected six which are only worth an 'Atish' or half a conkful. When I have collected the twelve vouchers I will let him have them, then he can have a really fantastic 'Atishoo'. The man in the 'Snuffery' says that it's very powerful stuff, and that before grandfather tries it he should take the plaster ducks down from over the mantelpiece otherwise they'll all migrate when he sneezes, whether they like it or not.

You said in your letter that you weren't sure how old grandfather was. There's an easy way of finding out — ask grandmother to count the wrinkles on one of his legs and divide by two.

Love
  Jimmy

Dear Jimmy

I am writing to you as you can probably tell from the words on the paper. I told your grandmother what you said about finding out how old grandfather was by counting the wrinkles on one of his legs and dividing by two. She did this and got a shock when she found out that he was 654. She then realised that he still had his long Johns on and she had forgotten to iron them, so there were a lot more wrinkles than there should have been.

We had a lovely birthday party, your grandfather had a grand time as all the men who were taken prisoner with him during the war came – the Governor let them out for the night. After a few drinks your uncle John got all romantic and he blew down your aunt Norah's left ear. Her tights inflated and she floated out throught the kitchen window – fortunately a bus was passing at the time and a man who was sitting upstairs managed to grab hold of her by the leg. She was quite happy and singing at the top of her voice, 'Do you want your old lobby washed down' as I took her home on the end of a piece of string. Your grandfather wanted to make a speech but every time he went to stand up he banged his head on the table. It was a night to remember.

Love
  Mammy

JIMMY: Mammy!

MAMMY: You don't sound like her.

JIMMY: It's me!

MAMMY: What do you want, Mr Itsme?

JIMMY: It's me, Jimmy.

MAMMY: Who?

JIMMY: Your son, Jimmy!

MAMMY: It's a terrible line.

JIMMY: This book's full of them. How's dad?

MAMMY: He's gone out looking for work.

JIMMY: That's good.

MAMMY: That's bad.

JIMMY: How do you mean?

MAMMY: He's wearing a blindfold.

JIMMY: He's lost his job with British Rail.

MAMMY: He's very upset.

JIMMY: It's a shame. Forty years welding the crusts onto the meat pies.

MAMMY: The shop didn't have the string vests you asked for.

JIMMY: Don't worry about it.

MAMMY: I haven't let you down. I've sent you two sprout nets and put sleeves in for your arms.

JIMMY: I'll have to dash. There's a man outside waiting to ring for an ambulance.

MAMMY: How do you know he wants an ambulance?

JIMMY: He's carrying his head in a carrier bag.

MAMMY: When are you coming home?

JIMMY: You said when dad's finished redecorating my room.

MAMMY: I'll see you in about fifteen years. Bye.

JIMMY: Bye, mammy!

Dear Jimmy

We had a terrible shock during the night, a man broke into the house while we were in bed. He ran off when your father had the presence of mind to collapse. A man came from the security firm and he advised us to have a rubber alarm bell fitted as we have nothing worth pinching. A lot of houses have been broken into around here lately. A man broke into Miss Tasker the spinster lady's house last Monday night, she sent for the police on Thursday afternoon. The police asked Miss Tasker if she wanted to charge the man and she said 'No' as the man had already given her a tenner to ring for the police. A young feller tried to hold up the Post Office last week and I don't think he'd ever done a robbery before. He put the balaclava helmet on back to front, ran into the fish and chip shop next door with a baseball bat and fell head-first into the hot fat. He is now in police custody full of remorse and very crispy. It's a terrible world we're living in.

Love
  Mammy

Dear Mammy

I was sorry to hear about the trouble you've been having at home, it's even worse here. This afternoon we had a police raid at the television studio. They didn't find anything, they were looking for jokes. Patrick Moore who does *The Sky at Night* had his bike stolen the other night. He wasn't very happy because he had to get home in a hurry and it's a long walk to Venus.

I've got some great news for you, Mammy. You should be hearing from a man who wants to print all our letters in a book and sell them. He said he'd call and see you about the idea, you might make a lot of money. Let me know what happens.

Love
  Jimmy

Dear Jimmy

The man did call about putting the letters into a book and selling them. I didn't realise that there was so much money involved. According to the man he wouldn't be surprised if the sales of the book would give me enough money to buy that one luxury I've always wanted – a new floor cloth. Your father says that if the book does make a lot of money it'll be 'Goodbye' to the job at the Iron Foundry. I hope so as I never did like working there.

Love
  Mammy

Dear Mammy

Things are beginning to move quite quickly now. The man from the publishing factory has said that they are going to put the letters into a book just as soon as they have been translated into English. I'm very excited. I said to the man, 'If people buy the book I might become another George Bernard Priestley.' He said, 'Shaw.' I said, 'I'm positive.' If the book is a success I will probably write my autobiography. I'll write that one myself. I hope you're as thrilled as I am.

Love
  Jimmy

Dear Jimmy

Things are happening so quickly I don't know whether I'm on my head or my bunion plaster. A man came to the house to interview me for the television. Unfortunately they couldn't bring the cameras into the house as they won't work off gas. He wanted to know all about when you were a youngster. I told him that you ran away from home when you were two as you felt that you weren't getting anywhere. Your father doesn't seem in the slightest bit intersted, he never was much of a reader. As you know, he wouldn't join the library because he thought he might have to pass a medical. Do you know for certain sure that they are going to put these letters into a book?

Love
  Mammy

Dear Mammy

The letters are definitely going to be made into a book that will appeal to people of all ages from five to five and a half. The man from the publishing factory brought the contract around this morning. He told me it was just the usual sort of a contract and not to bother reading the small print at the bottom. He said it would only be a waste of time as it was written in Javanese in invisible ink. He's a nice man so I signed it. He wants to get the book on the shelves in the shop before Christmas so that people will know what to buy for relatives they haven't got much time for. It's a nice thought.

Love
  Jimmy

Dear Jimmy

Since news got out that I'm going to be in a book
I've become a bit of a local celebrity. Last Saturday
I was invited to judge a Baby Competition.
Unfortunately I left my specs at home and there was
a bit of a barney amongst the mothers when I gave
first prize to a six-month-old cockerspaniel. Your
grandmother is overjoyed with the book—she says
it has stopped the kitchen table from wobbling as it
just fits under the leg. I might buy half a dozen myself
and shove them under your father and see if they'll
do the same for him.

Love
  Mammy

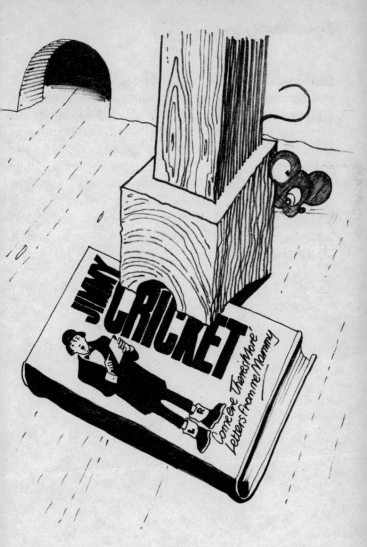

Dear Mammy

It's a wonderful thing to see our letters in a book on sale in the shops. I owe it all to you, Mammy. We all owe it to our Mammys. I hope that this isn't . . .

THE END

P.S. To the person looking at this book in the shop now. If you are just flicking through the pages to pass the time would you mind putting the book back as the man next to you might have a few bob. Thank you.

P.P.S. If you find anything in this book that makes you laugh would you let me know as I'd be very grateful.

Please note that under the terms of the authors and publishers act of 1365 this book cannot under any circumstances be used for swotting bluebottles.

If you have ever written letters to your mammy or had letters sent to you by your mammy, why don't you get in touch with the publisher of this book who is at the moment enjoying a long stay in a rubber room in a big house in Berkshire.

The following hilarious humour titles are also available from Star Books

JIMMY CRICKET
Come 'ere – There's More

Letters from me Mammy

Illustrated by
PAUL TREVILLION

Dear Mammy

I'm a bit worried about these digs I'm in. I asked the landlady how much the rent was per week. She said she didn't know, no one's ever stayed that long.

I said, 'Give me a room and a bath.' She said, 'You can have the room all right but you'll have to bath yourself.'

I'm off to look for a job tomorrow.

Love
  Jimmy

ISBN 0 352 32109 1   £1.99

Spike Milligan

A DUSTBIN OF MILLIGAN

My son has asked me to write this, he is a good boy, and very kind to his mother. It was never more than flesh wounds he gave me. He bought me a washing machine for his birthday, but every time I got in, the paddles nearly beat me to death, oh how we laughed. He is a good boy and kind to his mother. We make big bonfires for him, but he never goes in. He climbed a tree for his summer holiday. He likes climbing trees. We gave him one for Christmas. He fell off. Oh how we laughed. He is a good boy and kind to his mother. Oh how we laughed.

His Mother

✗

Her Mark

ISBN 0 352 30629 7   £1.99

A BOOK OF BITS
OR
A BIT OF A BOOK

by Spike Milligan

A BOOK OF BITS OR A BIT OF A BOOK is more than a Bit of a Book and not just a Book of Bits. On the other hands, it is not a bitty book and it has its 'booky' bits. However . . . it really is impossible to describe a Spike Milligan opus, but if you have read *The Little Pot Boiler* and *A Dustbin of Milligan* this new one is the book for you (and it's for you even if you haven't).

ISBN 0 352 30626 2   £1.35

Spike Milligan

THE BEDSIDE MILLIGAN

The Bedside Milligan
The Milliside Bedman
The Sideigan Millibed
The Millside Bedagain
The Milligad Bedsign

Whichever way you put it this book can be dipped into at any suitable interval and you may come out with an uproarious lump, a lump in the throat, or a thoughtful lump.

Whichever it is it will be beneficial, or so say the publishers from experience.

so

BUY THIS BOOK
IT'S GOOD FOR YOU
AND ANYBODY ELSE

But for God's sake buy it!

*PUBLISHER'S NOTE
*IN FACT EVERY NOTE

ISBN 0 352 30627 0   £1.99

JIMMY CRICKET

☐ 0 352 32109 1   Come 'ere—There's More   £1.99

SPIKE MILLIGAN

☐ 0 352 30626 2   **A Book of Bits**   £1.35

☐ 0 352 30629 7   **A Dustbin of Milligan**   £1.99

☐ 0 352 30627 0   **The Bedside Milligan**   £1.99
